CONCEPTUAL SELLING-PART-1

An Interview with Sales Mangers and Sales Employees

Dr. Amit Phillora

The book is dedicated to my parents and all sales employees who were part of sales interview program.

Book Title Copyright © 2019 by Dr Amit Phillora. All Rights Reserved.
Diary Number: 9761/2019-CO/L

All rights reserved. No part of this book may be reproduced in any form or by any electronic or mechanical means including information storage and retrieval systems, without permission in writing from the author. The only exception is by a reviewer, who may quote short excerpts in a review.

Cover designed by KDP Cover Creator

This book is a work of fiction. Names, characters, places, and incidents either are products of the author's imagination or are used fictitiously. Any resemblance to actual persons, living or dead, events, or locales is entirely coincidental.

Dr. Amit Phillora
Visit my website
amazon.com/author/dr.amitphillora

Kindle Direct Publishing

ISBN-13 : 9781096277361

CONTENTS

Chapter-1 : Introduction to Conceptual Sales 5
Chapter2: Sales Clock Diagrammatic Representation of Sales Clock 7
Chapter3: Basic Analytics of Sales 10
Chapter-3 : Sales Person and His Working 13
Chapter-4: Principles of Sales 16
Chapter 5:Salesman Life in Sales World 21
Chapter 6: 26
How to Loose a Sale? 26
Chapter-6 : Role of Tele-Sales 29
Bibliography 32

Chapter-1: Introduction to Conceptual Sales

Sales & Salesperson

Well, every sales person owns a sales clock with 3 important hands Sales Numbers, Sales Pipelines & Sales Forecasting. Till this clock is ticking salesperson has a room to have a smile on his face. Sales is an gamble, as even if you so sure that the deal is coming in as it has all your hard work and every possible modes to be successful but even then it has a probability of not happening . Well we can also address sales with number game for sale person. Till the numbers are coming in with the active running of sales clock the sales person is successful but when this numbers stops and the clock stops running the sales person faces the toughest time of his/her life, as the management is least bothered with your efforts and hard word you have putted to get a deal as it all in vein if the deal is not coming in and you will be held responsible as in a sales organization we cant blame our clients even if they back out in 11th hour.

But at the same time a salesperson is not just known for generating sales and revenue for the sales organization. He is also responsible for generating sales leads that is acquiring new clients to his/her organization. As we know that a salesperson is the mirror of the company at which the client can see his image of benefits and problem-solving solutions. So it's very important for a sales person to leave a very correct impression of the clients specially with those who has never done business with them. A salesperson must be very processional and must be a very good listener and must have a personality which compels his clients to meet him or draw attention towards him.

To be a salesperson or sales executive one need to follow the following things:

- Attractive Personality and good Communication Skills;
- Professional attitude;
- Punctual and must know time management;
- Must be polyglot[i]
- Must have good listening and understanding power;
- Salesperson must be good in Logical and Analytical Analysis;
- Must have learning attitude and should posse's leadership qualities;
- Must know everything about the company and line of products.

These are some of the qualities which I feel a salesperson must have and no compromises must be done in this.

Note: "A Salesperson must be prepared for worst situations also and must be capable enough to come out of it with a smiling face."

Selling is an art, and which can't be mastered or thought to someone.

We can give guidelines to be successful but it's up to the salesperson how they implement these guidelines for developing a successful graph of his or her sales career.

Chapter 2: Sales Clock

Diagrammatic Representation of Sales Clock

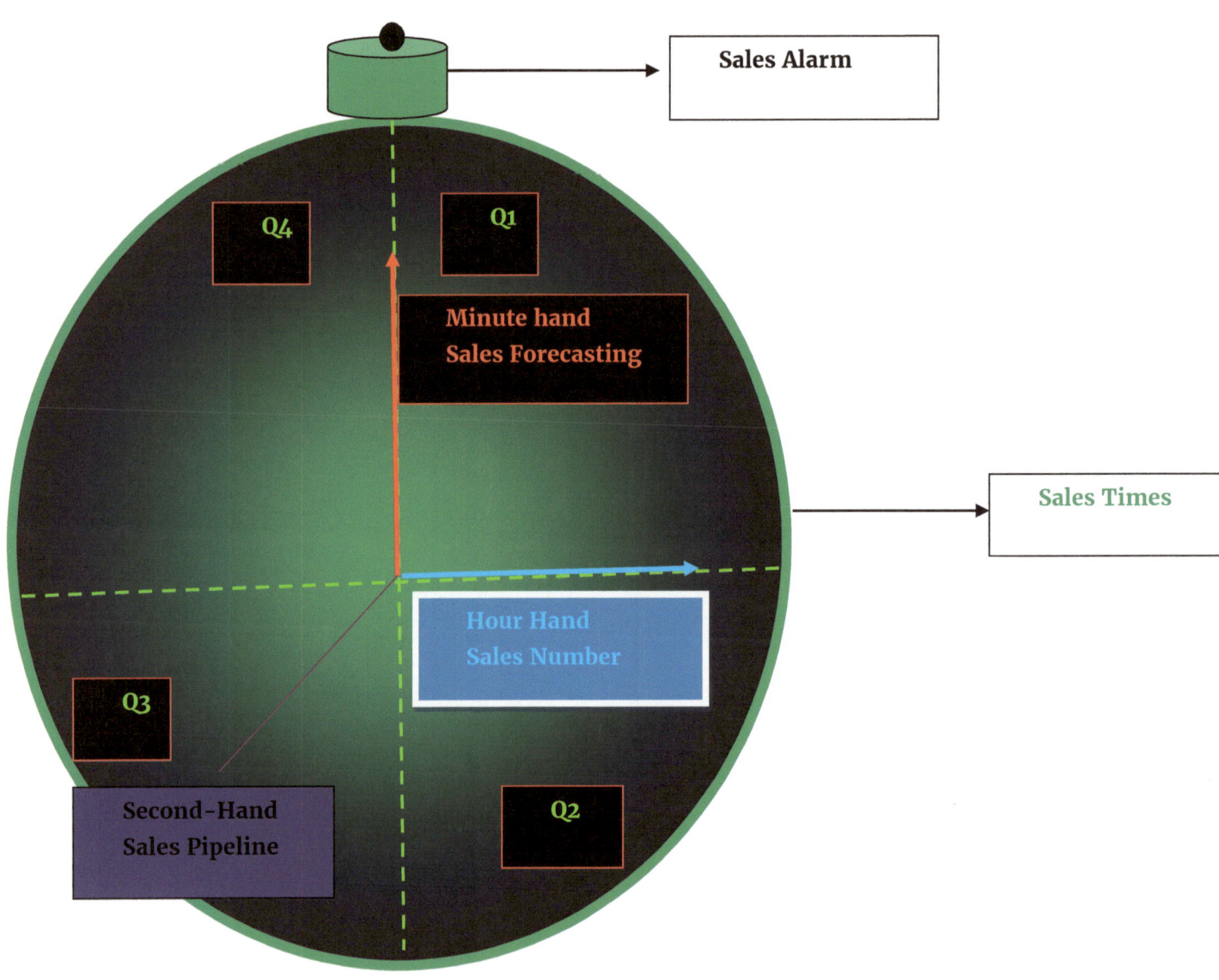

Components of Sales Clock

1) **3 hands of clock :**
    i) **Second hand as Sales Pipeline:** The most important weapon that a salesperson has is sales pipeline. The stronger the pipeline the stronger the chances are of getting sales out of it and the weaker pipeline the lesser chances of getting sales. To generate sales, you need to have a valid sales file. As the second passes the sales pipeline must be increasing as it the fuel of your sales car.

    ii) **Minute Hand as Sales Forecasting**: As we know that after completion of 1 round of second hand it gives a time of 60 seconds & this 60 seconds makes a minute, means that a sales person must be experienced enough to know at what client he need to spend time or which client is to be left .after spending so much of time in generating his pipe line he must be knowing what are his/her closures, based on this he can divide his Pipe line into following format :

    a) **Hot Leads:** These are the leads for immediate closures, where the salesperson knows that this deal is coming in very shortly

    b) **Warm Leads:** These are the leads at which the salesperson is actually working on. They got warm because of some small problems like pricing or some other problems and will take little more time to get closed

    c) **Cold Leads:** These are the leads which got cold due to certain reasons and are not coming in short time span. It can happen when the prospect has bought product from your competitor or when he is facing some financial crisis or a shut shop of business.

    iii) **Hour Hand As Sales Number** : As we know in an clock when minute hand completes one round it completes one complete hour & this hour consists of seconds and minutes as :
    [60 second (pipeline) makes 1 minute (sales forecast) & 60 minutes makes 1 hour (sales number).]. Well after working hard on pipeline and forecasting we will get our sales for sure.

   Note: If we assume this hypothesis of generating a lead in very second and get it forecasted in 60 seconds, we will surely get the sale in next 1 hour. This can only be possible if salesperson uses his sales experience in right direction with 100% focus on his/her pipe lines.

2) **Sales Alarm** : After doing proper sales forecasting a sales person must trigger the alarm of his sales clock as he know that this is the time when the sale is coming in. that's getting the sales in correct time. As this ringing of this alarm on the sales number is generated.

3) **Sales Times**: a salesperson has a sales clock which has a sales time of 12 months that is 1 year. This sales time is divided into 4 sales quarters which are represented as Q1, Q2, Q3, Q4. The sales clock start ticking from the 1st quarter itself. During this period a sales person is assigned with certain target (Q1`,Q2`,Q3`&Q4`) which needs to complete at the end of ever quarter to complete the sales clock successfully.

Chapter3: Basic Analytics of Sales

Formulas Related to Quarterly and Annual Sales

General formula for calculating sales time and sales target

Sales Time: Q1+Q2+Q3+Q4.
Sales Target: Q1`+Q2`+Q3`+Q4`

CALCULATION OF SUCCESS RATIO OF SALESPERSON

By watching this sales clock which is mechanically controlled & governed by the sales managers and top sales professionals at higher grade the success ratio of salesperson is calculated.

For e.g.
Balanced Salesperson:
Q= Q1` at (q1) +Q2` at (q2) +Q3` (q3) +Q4`at (q4)

Where,
Q = Annual Sales Target.
Q1`=Quarter 1 Sales Target
Q2`= Quarter 2 Sales Target
Q3`= Quarter 3 Sales Target
Q4`= Quarter 4 Sales Target

q1, q2, q3&q4 are the respective times of the quarters Q1`,Q2`,Q3`&Q4`.

Now let the total annual target be 1 that is Q=1. It means that salesperson has to complete 0.25 of his targets every quarter & if he is able to do it then he will be called as successful sales person. i.e.

Q=.0.25+.25+.25+.25=1
That's equation is a balanced equation that's the given targets are completed by the salesperson.

Such kind of salesperson is called as a **balanced or average salesperson** (Q=1) who just completes his targets. But suppose **Q≠1**, Then 2 things can happen
- ❖ Q<1
- ❖ Q>1

Condition 1 when **Q<1**, then salesperson is called as a failure i.e. is sales clock is lagging behind & is not but working properly. Salesperson following under these criteria are called as **weak salesperson**

Condision2: but if **Q>1** then the sales clock is ticking very good as the in this condition extra sales are coming which shows our hypothesis of generating more leads and able to convert those leads into prospects and closures is working due to which our sales clock is running fast and alarms are triggered before the completion sales time resulting more sales and profits to the company. Such salespersons are the driving force of the sales organization. They can be called as **Sales Leaders**.

So, we can say that a sales organization has 3 categories salespeople:

- **Week Salesperson**: They are the people who are failing in meeting their sales targets & require attention by the higher authorities to understand why their clock & sales alarm not working properly.
- **Average Salesperson**: They are the salespeople who just work for completing their job. They never fail in their work but looses the zeal once reaches or complete their target as they lose their focus. These people need proper guidance and regular monitoring so that they get improvised and comes in the category of sales leaders.
- **Sales Leaders:** They are the top category salesperson for them sales is like and passion. They give their 100% or even more to achieve their targets. These people never sit idle and keep generating their pipelines and focus lots of time in Sales Pipeline & Sales Forecasting technique. These people need appreciations and authorities to take decisions which make them more motivated to perform better than the best. It's always advised that sales leaders must be made mentors for weak salesperson so that they can work out properly and comes out for a solution beneficial for both of them & also for the team.

Chapter-3: Salesperson and His Working

The Story of Salesperson and Sales Pipeline

Before we understand what a sale pipeline its always important to understand what is a sales lead file.

Sales lead file is the list of leads or prospects given to salesperson for doing sales. From this sales lead the leads which are forecasted for closures are called as **sales pipelines**

Game of Priorities

You (Salesperson) might have always observed that client meets you properly and listens to you and also shows interest in buying product or services from you but then never buys product/services from. He never replies to your mails, phone calls etc. you may think what went wrong, you contacted the correct person and he showed lots of interest in buying your product & services then why is he behaving like this? Then you will be questioned by your higher authorities as this lead is being forecasted by you only. This will forces you to give some excuses to the authorities as you don't know what went wrong, as such clients will always listen to you and will also respect you but will never buy product and services from you. ==This is called as "Full Plate Syndrome".==

Such a client once shows interest to you & without identifying you explain him everything in proper way like any other sales call, the client backs out as he thinks that he doesn't have space in his plate to put the thing in his plate and will say he has a full plate. Now, once you got to know that your client is suffering from **full plate syndrome**, prepare a ==Secondary Plate== for him at which you put your product and services based on his priorities and show this plate to him. Now its obvious that once primary plate is full new things can't be added to it but there are always chances that certain things can be replaced from client's full plate and your products from secondary plate can be adjusted there.

Now let's take an example which will explain you the concept. You have a tight schedule tomorrow and you have prepared a scheduled meeting with you clients & your 1st meeting is at 9.30 Am Sharp. But before you go to bed & your boss calls you & ask you meet him at conference room as he wants to discuss about your performance appraisal and salary increment at 9.30 Am. For sure you will attend this meeting as at that time your priority is your promotion and sales hike, so you will cancel your meetings. So, it's all the game of identifying your client's priority.

Saying that client is not interested and not picking up calls etc. try to understand what his most prior things is are in his business and then present your product and services accordingly, if you will do this there are very less chances of sales failure. All you must be **"Stay in the game"** just keep following your client and even if he didn't take services from you keep providing them the solutions. Keep a track on their business and their business problems& keep sending them the new paper clippings, sites , video clippings and problem solution related presentations which could actually help them to come out of the business crises, this is give an positive impression of yours to them and whenever they will buy services they will buy it from you only.

S.W.O.T. Analysis

When a sales lead file is given to a salesperson, it's always advised that a detailed SWOT analysis of the lead file must be done so that a sales person can identify the hot leads and prospects out of it.

It's well known that a salesperson is always assigned with a Sales Territories and will get lead of these sales regions only. A demographic study of the sales territory must be done and then find out the target audiences and this can be done by identifying

1. **Strengths**: Try to understand the business of your clients. Try to find out their strengths and positive points like their financial status, their annual turnover, etc. but this is if you are targeting the companies of these territories. But if your product requires common people then you need to do the demographic study & based on that you need to segment your sales territory and understand in which your segment your product falls and out which who all can afford to buy your product & there after target them.

2. **Weakness:** After studying your territory try to understand why sales are failing in your region. Try find out the problems faced by your target audiences. once you understood what the problem is try to bring out solutions in such a way which differentiates you from your competitors i.e. don't do what other sales people are doing or had been doing, do something different which should draw attention of your target audiences towards you and once you have done this then you have almost won the half battle. As now you know what their problems are and what unique and different solutions.

3. **Opportunity:** Once you have identified your clients Strengths & Weakness you can easily create opportunities for yourself i.e. you can sell your products to them. Even if currently they are not interested in buying as of now you can keep in track to them, so that you can keep yourself updated regarding the sales opportunities with them. Once opportunity comes you can grab it as you already ready with the problems and solutions for them, it will be easy for you to sell your product to them in comparison to your competitors.

4. **Threats:** Make your target audiences aware of problems which they can face by not buying the product from them. Also tell the ease of problem solving by buying your products and services.

Strength	Weakness
• Financial status of target audience. • interested at your products	Reason of failure of their sales of their products
Opportunities Doing sales based of healthy professional relationship which you created with them.	Threats Explaining the Importance of getting this sale done and how it will impact their business if this sale didn't happen.

Lead files

Salesman

Note:" Once correct SWOT analysis for your lead-file is done you can start your sales clock."

Chapter-4: Principles of Sales

Sales & Its Principles in corporate world

a) Once told is not always sold:

Well as we know that, **"telling is not selling"**. Explaining about your product and services to your client doesn't means that your selling the product to them or once you have briefed them about your products and services the client will buy it.

It must be very clear in the salesmen's mind that client is not that much interested in your company and its product services, all he wants the proper solution for his current business problems.

Once you have listened to the problem of your client, bring practical solutions in front of his so that you can hold his attention towards you.

This can be done by" **client problem identification**" & not by explaining your product and services.

Now how to detect the client's problem?
It's very simple; just ask high valued questions related his business issues. Let the answers be known to you , once you do it you will able to understand your clients problems and you can easily bring out the solutions and can get the sales deal in. By answering those high valued questions will bring week points of their business in front of them and providing an different unique successful solutions will always help you in giving an positive impression in front of your clients and you will get an successful sales.

b) Don't stop at your 1st failure:
It is always important for a salesperson to keep changing his approaches to make his self as different salesperson in comparison to other salesmen & these different approaches must be practiced until unless success is not achieved. Most of the salespeople know this but still do such mistakes. They prefer to try old and tried sales techniques and are afraid of using new, different and untried sales techniques.

Let's take an e.g.
A family stays in a hotel room. The hotel room has filter water facility for drinking water. The filter was empty, so the family complained at the reception and the filter was filled immediately but again after 2-3 days same problems arised. Again, the complaint was launched but no one took action that time. So, the family went to reception and asked from where we can buy water. The receptionist showed a shop in front of their hotel. After that she asked why you want drinking water to be bought, we provide filter water free of cost. The family said see the complain number 23, from past 2 days we are not getting water so maybe we thought we need to pay something for buying water. After that day they never faced any room service related problem during their stay and their filtered water was changed and refilled on regular basis.

If one approach fails a salesperson must always be ready for Plan B & he should be smart enough to switch to plan B easily.

c) Learn to walk before you start running.

Salesmen must know that sales are never got by chasing it. It's not always easy to get sales, a lot of hard-work and lost of focus is required. Once you (salesmen) get a lead he must not immediately look for closures. A new sales-lead is just like a newborn baby who doesn't know how to crawl then how can you expect him to run.

Mostly sales work with principle of **"crawl, walk and run"**, just like a small baby.

- **Crawl or problem identification:** The first step a salesman is supposed to do is problem identification, so that he can prepare himself in front of his client. As a buyer is never interested in what you are and to which company you belong to, he is much interested in the fact what that what you have to give which can benefit him or his business.

- **Walk or Providing solutions:** Once you have correctly identified the problems of your clients like what stopping him to buy services from your company then you can prepare your self with an attractive presentations with facts and figures which will have all the solutions for his problems. Once you are done with this you can ask for a meeting with your client. Don't talk to him as a sales guy. Just provide him solutions which are very much different from your competitors and try to gather more information from your clients that what is the practical issues is he looking for and go ahead with the profession discussion with him. Try to be a good listener.

- **Run or closures:** Now once you have done problem identification and their solutions to all of the problems which your clients were facing you can grab active feedbacks from them and based on that you can expect your closures with them. This will help you in adjusting your sales clock and based on it you can set sales alarm (correct forecasted time) and get your deal in.

This is what new sales lead is to be done, then only you can expect to close that sales lead.

d) **Don't rush on the calls**

A salesperson must understand that it's all about business which bought them together in this professional relation as you are selling your product to them as they need your product. Salesperson must always be focused and bold enough to talk straight to your buyers. It requires lots of focus, discipline and courage to talk straight to your clients straight as no one has time to waste on non business talks so sales person must be straight enough to say ," I understand your situation before putting together information when would be the good time to schedule a 20 minute calls. And these 20 minutes will be the time where you can make this client as prospect client or loose the client. Always take an appointment from your clients before getting into sales-business talks, as you and your client both need to spend some time to get this business deal done.

e) **Just do it**

Mishandling of cold calling: Most of the salesmen know how to handle cold call but fear of failures and rejections stops them from taking quicker actions towards his cold clients resulting in mismanagement or neglecting of his cold clients.

A salesperson must understand that," no one is perfect in this world", & should carry the attitude of," failure is the next step for success", it means that don't run away from your cold leads. All they need to work on cold leads and take quick actions before the lead dies.

It's not necessary that a sales talk will always end in sales closures, sometimes things don't work as we had planned , so such things must be cleared before only as the more you delay the more chances you create to loose the deal , so why not face it and finish it once for all.

f) **Outside the theory of books**

Most of the experienced salespeople know all the theoretical knowledge and they don't have time to get into the theory of sales and then prove them weather which theory of sales will work for them. All they want is a way out to get the sales in their bags of sales. like for example a salesperson based on his experience makes some strategies now instead of applying them directly they seek knowledge that weather these strategies will help them to get some sales in or not. They go with the attitude of ,"**Yeah I know this** but tell me weather this will help me or not ", else no matter how good and attractive a sales strategy looks like if its not going to give some benefit is of no use to sales guys.
Let's take a case at which a salesperson looses his/her client in just 5 seconds or even less then that.

It's a call between you and decision maker. The call starts:

Me: Greetings to you Mr. DSC Mkr (Name of the person). This is amit from xyz limited.

Dsc Mkr: Yes, tell me how I can help you.

Me: self-introduction and company profile and product services that your going to offer is spoken of by you.

Here where you can gain the attention or loose the attention of your client. The moment the decision maker recognizes that's its an ordinary sales call he will loose all interest and can interrupt you in between and gives you a time to call back you again and that time never comes as he will never attend your call again.
To avoid such situations be brief and to the point like what is the purpose of your call and how can you help them in their business. Take some examples of your clients who all got benefited by you and your services. Your call or meeting should be in keeping your client mind and situation in your mind. Don't make it as sales call, just talk about business and its solutions. That will hold the attention of your client. Always remember the model AIDA.

That's, **Attention, Interest, Desire, Action** that's all your client want. Place the 4 keys properly in-front of your clients and see how the cold leads turns into warm leads and the warm leads to hot leads leading to successful sales closures.

Chapter 5: Salesman Life in Sales World
Pattern of his working i.e. Working Style of a Salesperson

Salesman Life.

Motivation plays a very important role in salesperson life. Positive motivation helps a salesperson to develop in positive sense and helps him to grow; whereas no motivation or negative motivation reduces the sales person life.

Here are four ideas by Sir Kelly (a famous sales leader.)

- **Do Something Different**: It's always advised to salesperson to come up with new sales techniques rather than trying old sales techniques. Once these new sales trick click successful will show you the path of success.
- **Join a master mind**: You can join a group of successful sales leaders, where you can discuss your problems regarding sales failures, based on their experiences they will suggest you the solutions for your problems & by applying their techniques who knows you get lucky in your closures. You can also discuss bottle neck with them. Bottle necks are such cases which are on the verge of closures but due some very minute problems are lying in your pending lists. Buy getting feedback on your bottle neck cases you will understand what the problems are and how can be they be solved.
- **Network**: Most of salespeople forget their clients after getting sales with them, that's not right. You can learn many things from them and anyhow doing a sale with is not one-time business you would like to retain such clients with your company. You can get good reference leads from them also you can also take tips from them that how they are running their business successfully, this will develop a special relation between you two and this will increase your network & sales territory. You can seek advices from them based on their feedbacks you can improvise your self and again present your self in front of your new clients. This will increase your probability to get sales.
- **Get out of sales for some time**: Working round the clock makes a salesperson stressed out and often gets de-motivated. A salesperson must have a social life also i.e. he must always take some time off from his sales clock and give some to his hobbies and family, this will refresh him and lots of positive energy will be gained during this time.

Generation of valid lead

Salesmen has one more important thing to do is new client's acquisitions. That's bringing those clients who are very new to this business. This will also help then in increasing their sales lead file. Well apart from net surfing or news paper ads etc its always advisable to ask for references from your existing clients as they may be having lots of knowledge regarding the market situation and will be able to give you some valid leads who will be definitely be aware of your products and services and you can expect quick responses from them.

According **Mr. Kelly** there are 3 key points which can help a salesperson in generating a valid sales lead:

(a) **Be Clear:** While talking to your existing clients you must e very clear that sir/madam do you know at your knowledge that are looking for similar kinds of product and services so that we can also help the them like we helped you. You must also inform that you are looking for leads which are for immediate closures.

(b) **Be Consistent:** You cannot ask on regular basis for new leads from your existing clients, you need to as consistently to everyone who stays in your business contact.

(c) **Set It Up:** During your conversation tell them that your business largely depends on referral leads, so kindly do refer his name to your other people who are looking for the same kind of services, make them feel important by saying your word to them will help them to grow in their business the way you grew with us.

Eyes & Ears Open, Mind Attentive & Mouth Close

Focus is one of the most important weapons of the salesmen. As we know that salesperson must be a very good listener and must pay attention towards the client's wordings and problems and must only open his mouth when it's required. His mind must always be focused and must be full of problem definition and their solutions. The mind set must always be prepared with most asked **FAQ's (Frequently Asked Questions).**

The salesmen must be much focused, and his focus is shown by the type of high valued questions that he will put in-front of his prospect. Generally, you may ask questions like:

(a) Are you interested in this?
(b) Do you want to see it?
(c) Can I Show you?
(d) Would you like me to tell you about it?

These are not high valued questions and are baseless leading your warm prospect to convert into one of your cold or dead clients, who may never buy services from you.

Buyers and decision makers are very much interested in their agenda, they are least bothered with selling agenda & that's why often ignores sales calls as they don't find any solutions of their problems coming out of it. So, you must keep the buyer's agenda with yourself when your in meeting with your prospects. You must ask high valued questions like:

(a) Tell me what's your current situation?
(b) How this situation is affecting your business like your ROI, profits, company projects, financial status etc.
(c) How is it affecting your financial strength of your company?
(d) If this problem is solved what would you like to do in your extra time?

Salesmen must be much focused and should spend his sales time only on those clients whom he thinks potential. To leave a positive impact on decision makers a salesman must talk to them in straight forward way. The communication must be short and productive as both you and they have time to listen all sales talks and stories. The high valued questions will differentiate you from your fellow salespersons or your competitors.

Wrap It All

It's always to take a quick recap by you (Salesmen) before you end your sales talk or meeting. This will give a very good impression to your prospect and will also help him to recall the entire discussion.

Due to these four things will happen:

(a) The client will think that you listening to him & give him the impression that you are here to help him out at your terms and conditions.
(b) It will force you pay 100% attention to your clients talks.
(c) It clears all the gaps between you and will help you to understand his problem definition clearly and once it is done you can work accordingly.
(d) A quick recap will help your client to know what exactly he spoke to you and what is it he exactly looking at.

Why the decision makers don't talk you

It's very simple, they don't have time to listen sales stories and not at all interested in what you are and what your company deals with. All they want is how their business problems can be solved. Most of the salespeople fail to understand that and keeps giving excuses that the decision makers are not listening to you. If they are not willing to listen you, you make them listen to you as you are here to help him. You should be contacting them with full preparations and must posses some things which will hold them to listen to you and call you by themselves only for buying solutions from you.

Negotiation

As a salesperson you might have herd this question many times, "What's your best price". Now, to grab the sale quickly some salespeople drop their prices and give them good discounts that are wrong because of the following:

(a) Firstly, by selling your product & services at lower price you are reducing the profit margin for your company. Image the happiness of you and your manager if you can sell the product at price which is more then the MRP price of the product and services.

(b) Secondly, if you quote huge discounts to your clients easily, he may think that he can further negotiate from you and then can compare it with your competitors. In this case 99% chances are them to lose the deal as at this time the client will get to stuck on a price which you will not be able to provide, and you will lose a very good deal. So, you must not give discounts very quickly. Use discounts only when you think they are required & discounts must be given in such a way that their must be enough room for further negotiations.

(c) For getting deals with good profit ranges a salesman must do following things:

- **Maintain eye to eye contact with your clients with a smile on your face.** When he asks the best price from you then always quotes 20% extra from the original price. This will show your confidence and will give an impression to your client that you have correctly quoted the price

- **On Sales Call:** If you are talking to your client then talk to him with full confidence as your voice will be representing your personality to him. Your voice must be aggressive and must be showing zeal that you are here to help him and solve his business problems. Your sales talks must be so impressive that the decision maker is bound to listen them.

Ask-Shut Up-Listen

Ask a question from your client and then shut-up and listen to your client even if you know the answer. Listen carefully what your client says and take it as the feedback & that's how you get your closures. Here I will tell you few of the high valued questions that can help you in getting sales closed successfully.

After you have given your presentation to your client, ask, **"Are you with me so far?"** you can also ask, **"How does that sound?"** or **"Do you see what I mean?"** & **"Does that make sense?"**

Once you give them a benefit which they can use asks," **How will you use it?"** ", could you use that", "would that work for you", or" would that be of benefit in your situation."

Again, listen to your client and ask," **Do you have any questions so far?"**

Trial closes are always good- **"does this seems to be kind of solutions you are looking for? Or "How is this sounding so far?" or with a smile in your voice, "Am I getting close to having a new client yet?"**

It sounds like you are chasing your client, but it will surely help you break the ice and will get your prospect to lower his/her guard.

Once you are done with your presentation, always ask," **What I haven't covered yet that is important to you?"**

This is one of the best ways to end your presentation! If they say that they don't have any questions to be asked, then you can ask for sales closures. If they have any questions answer them and after satisfying them, ask for closures.

The moral of the story is asking, shut-up & listen

Chapter 6: How to Loose a Sale?

Costly mistakes by salesmen: sometimes a small mistake can spoil a deal.

We can group such mistakes in 6 groups. If we keep these mistakes in our mind the probability of losing a sale will be reduced.

<u>These are mistakes are as follows:</u>

1) <u>Prospecting Mistakes:</u>

    - Time management: Not giving much time to your new clients. If you will not spend ample amount of time with your clients how will you understand them and close a deal with them.
    - Wrong judgment: talking to wrong person thinking him as decision maker.
    - Not giving proper Attention, Desire, and Interest & Actions to your prospects, this often results in losing your clients.
    - Note: Thinking that your client doesn't have interest in your product and allowing them to go away from you is one of the biggest mistakes a salesperson can ever make.

2) <u>Telephone mistakes:</u>
    - Not leaving your contact details behind. If you will not leave your contact details behind, then how will your clients get back to you?
    - Speaking so fast that the listeners fails to understand what exactly you want to convey. Such attitude often looses the interest of the decision makers as they fail to understand what exactly is conveyed to him and what is to be done with such a call.
    - Everyone is very particular for their names and if they are not pronounced properly it will give wrong impression and you can lose the deal.

3) <u>Crawling mistake:</u> These are the mistakes which are made by the salesperson at very 1st step of sales leads.
    - <u>Punctuality</u>: Time plays a key role here. Being late in your sales meeting or sales call can be the result of sales failure at it's very first stage.
    - <u>Wrong way to open your sales call:</u> You can lose a sales deal if you start your sales call with a lengthy explanation regarding your company and product lines. As discussed earlier your prospect is not all interested in what you are or what your company is about, they don't have time for this, all they want is what you have for them.
    - <u>Not listening to your clients properly</u>. By doing this your clients will feel neglected and will think that it's nothing but just another sales call & they will ignore you and your calls.

4) **Presentation Mistakes:**

- <u>Product value:</u> failed to explain the value of your product and its importance to your clients resulting in sales drop. Also, sometimes sales person don't present their product in-front of every client thinking that they won't buy product from them. This is one big mistake they do by letting your clients go away from you.
- <u>Risk Management:</u> you must always hide the risk factors, specially from the new clients. You must always show benefits which they can get from you not the drawbacks else due to these drawbacks you can lose your deals.
- <u>A.I.D.A. failure:</u> Not able to draw attention of your clients towards your presentations, due to this client loses interests towards you and your products and once interest is gone the desire to purchase your product & services automatically dies. And once your failed in this, there is no action possible as the client will say, "Sorry, I am not interested".

5). <u>Objection mistakes:</u>

- Taking objectives at face value.
- Defensive attitude towards objections.
- Not giving much time to understand the client's main objection.
- Thinking that price related objections are always related to prices and due to this neglecting, the objection due to which these price related objections are coming in their ways.

6). <u>Closing mistakes:</u>

- Lack of commitments for sales.
- Not asking the prospects for their business, after all you are here to do some business with and pull some sales out of them. So, after doing everything you don't ask for business from them then how will you get a sale from them.

Chapter-7 : Role of Tele-Sales

Sales & Cold Calling

Important points that a salesperson must keep in his mind are as follows:

1. **ABC (Always be closing):**

Salesmen must have the zeal of always be closure. I can and I will should be the attitude of the sales person. He must be focused and must have an attitude to convert a dead deal to a successful deal.

Right attitude at right time is very important in sales cycle. You can not sound like a begger, remember that you're here for business and business doesn't happen by begging. It's a give an take relation.

You are business associate who is here to help them out in their business and your designation is not less then them, so whenever you work with a client go with the attitude that you must get the deal.

No doubts and question marks must be there in your mind. Once you face your clients with such an impression, it will reflect your professionalism and dedication towards your work, it will show that your focus is 100% at your work and you are not here to waste his and your time. This confidence will always help you in becoming successful salesmen.

2. A salesperson must be S.M.A.R.T. i.e. **Self-Monitoring, Analysis** (analytically strong), **and Reporting Technology** (having appropriate knowledge about the product technology).

3. **Cold Calling & Salesmen**

There is a strange relation between salesmen and cold leads. Often sales men avoid working on cold leads, as they think that they are waste leads and to generate sales with such leads is very difficult and waste of time. They often forget that most of the business relies or depends on such leads. These clients are ready to buy your products, all they ask if a proper approach towards them.

The process of calling or working on cold/dead leads and converting them into warm or hot leads is called as cold calling.

Here are few reasons why salesmen hate cold calling:

- "I don't like rejections"
- I don't want to come across that I am desperate for business.
- I don't want to sound like telemarketer.
- I don't like to interrupt people at work.
- I don't know what to say.

These all some of the excuses a sales person may have before going on cold calling. I must say if you have an attitude of this kind a sale will never happen. To get a sale you need to have zeal to have it. "Only a hungry man can have food, a person who already had food will not be able to have it even if the dishes are from the list of his favorites." In similar way if you are hungry for some sale then only you will be able to get it else no matter what you do the sales is not coming in. the attitude, "I want this sale and I must get it ", will help you in cracking such dead leads.

A salesmen hate cold-calling because:

1. Cold calling ask for hard work. (But I guess sales men get paid for this only.)
2. The need and desire for instant gratification.: I believe there are two types of people :
    - People who are waiting for rewards
    - People who wants their rewards now even though the pay off may be higher if they wait.

Well salesmen make many cold calls, sometimes such cases irritate them and sometimes they do get frustrated, but they don't understand the more they call the more they come close to their cold clients. Every "no" is always "no", the dedication and hard work make such "nos" to "yes". You need to understand that most of the cold clients says no just because they want to say no & there is nothing wrong with your approach, so don't get frustrated , the more number of cold calls you make the more you will improve in your sales skills. Slowly and steadily you will come close to your close to your cold clients and once you establish a relation with them it will be very easy for you to sell your product to them. All you must do is make as much as cold calls you can and always calculate your ratings, buy this you will also understand where you are going wrong. This will allow you to be innovative as you will try to implement new sales techniques & strategies and if they click you can apply on other of your warm or hot leads.

Let me summarize the sales process:

1. Make an appointment with yourself for 1 hour/day.
2. Make as many calls as possible during that hour.
3. Create a Master list (generating a warm pipeline).
4. Make your calls brief.
5. Work without interruption.
6. Call during prime time.
7. Don't quit.

Keep these points in mind. These points will increase the probability for getting sales.

"**Note: Remember,**"Selling cannot be taught or it cannot be learnt, you can sell something only when want to sell it." want are desires are strongest weapons and if you have them you can get whatever you want."

Bibliography

Personnel Interviews at monsterindia.com by top professionals

Categories:

Senior Managers (Top Management of Monsterindia.com, Hyderabad, India)

1. MD Asia Pacific : Mr. Arun Tadanki (Now MD for Yahoo.com) : On Line discussion on linkedin.com **Date 13 March 2008)**
2. India Operations Head: Mr. Sanjay Modi. **Date 13 Aug 2009**
3. Channel Sales Head Telecalls (Aquision and Retention): Mr. Atul Malhotra : Personal Interview **15 Jun 09**
4. Regional Sales Manager Telesales Acquisition hyd:Mr. Akash jain
5. Senior Training Manager at monster.com: Zach , **19th Sept 2008**
6. Senior Sales Manager PA Acquisition :Mr.Praneeth Marnani,**20th March 2009**
7. Senior Sales Manager Hyderabad Telesales: Mr. Auro Jyoti Patnaik. **21st March 2009**

Senior Account Managers At Monsterindia.com, Hyderabad , TeleSales

1. Sr Account manager :Veera Babu ,**22 September 2008**
2. Sr.Account manager : Nazeer , **22 September 2008**
3. Sr.Account Manager : Neeta Kasi **13,November 2008**
4. Sr. Account manager : Sujhata Mala , **14 November 2008**
5. Sr. Account Manager: Venketesh Mekhala ,**15 Nov 2008**
6. Sr Account Manager :Praveen ,**17 December 2008**
7. Sr. Account Manager :Pratap ,**18th November 2008**
8. Sr Account Manager Retension : **Mis Prassana ,19th Nov 2008**
9. Sr Account Manager Mr.Arif Shaddy Ecommerce :,**20 Dec 2008**

Senior Sales Executives At Monsterindia.com

1. Sr. Telesales Executive Banagalore : Mr.Subragshu Badhra ,**20th March 2009**
2. Sr. Telesales Executive Bangalore : Mis Deepika Nirmal,**21st march 2009**
3. Sr. Telesales Executive Bangalore : Mis Lavanya ,**22 march 2009**
4. Sr. Telesales Executive Bangalore : Misis Manjuri Rizawan,**1 Oct 2009**
5. Sr. Telesales Executive Chinnai,Hyderabad Telesale :Mis Anjum Amlani,**22nd June 2009**
6. Sr.Telsesales Eexutive;Field Sales Executive Bangalore: Fatima Taiyab,**23rd June 2009**
7. Sr. Telesales Executive Retension : Mis Swetha Kulkarni ,**26th Aug 2009**

Books :

1. Kotler, Phillips. (2004). Principles of Marketing ,11th Edition, New Delhi: Pearson Education
2. Ken Lord, Selling Ice to Eskimos
3. Rich Dad Poor Dad.

[i] Multilingual : Knows more than 2 languages

www.ingramcontent.com/pod-product-compliance
Lightning Source LLC
Chambersburg PA
CBHW041303180526
45172CB00003B/944